Level Two

gentle
GRAMMAR

An Adaptation of New Language Exercises for Primary Schools
by C. C. Long

PREFACE

(Excerpted and adapted from the original book.)

These exercises are based upon these principles:

1. That the child learns by example and practice: not by rules or theory.

2. That the habits of utterance which a child begins to form at the very outset will cling to him through life.

He should, therefore, before bad habits of speech and writing are formed, begin with the facts that lead up to general grammatical laws; not as ordinary textbooks require, with rules and definitions.

No examples of false syntax are given, because, so far as possible, we should not allow pupils to see or hear what is wrong in language. The children's mistakes in speaking and writing will be found ample for correction and illustration.

These exercises have been used in large graded schools with the most satisfactory results, and are now offered to teachers with the hope that they may be found useful in leading the "little ones" to correct expression of their thoughts in speaking and writing.

SECOND READER GRADE. — Pictures, choice stories, animals, letter-writing, etc., will be found valuable in language teaching. The oral statement of information obtained should precede the written.

The value of pictures as a means of cultivating *thought* and *expression* in children is not fully appreciated. Pictures awaken interest and convey ideas which the mind of young people can not grasp from simple print.

Introduction

And Instructions

I have observed that, **if not corrected early-on, some habits of poor grammar and spelling can become like permanent marker on the walls of a young child's mind.** Even though I agree heartily with the idea that children learn spelling and grammar best by reading and writing, my own children have needed more specific instruction. However, I'm not willing to overburden them with a complete English program in every grade. This repetition of the same information year-after-year kills the love of language in children.

I needed to find a program that was:

- **Something I could put on "auto pilot"**

- **Quick (for kids who already had trouble sitting still for reading and math)**

- **Not technical**

- **Cheap and easy to put together (not too much printing, cutting, pasting, etc., etc., etc.)**

Early-on I discovered *Simply Grammar*, an expanded version of Charlotte Mason's *First Grammar Lessons*. However, the work was meant to be done orally, which was too much work for a woman juggling children at six different levels at the same time.

Finally, I stumbled upon Dollar Homeschool in *The Old Schoolhouse* magazine. This company specializes in collecting school books from times past and making them available in digital form for modern use. These materials were written before the Progressive education movement in America, a time before humanism and its psychobabble began to rule the way children were taught.

Included on one of the CD's from Dollar Homeschool was a collection of grammar books, and in particular two which I found very interesting. These were written by a person by the name of C. C. Long and were entitled *New Language Exercises for Primary Schools* part one and part two (I like to refer to them as "Long's Language"). **As I read through them I became more and more excited; this was finally the answer, the tool that would help fill the gap and turn my beginning readers into confident, competent writers!**

For one thing, the first lessons are not about nouns and verbs. There is actually very little mentioned in the first book about grammar at all, although grammar is the subject. Instead, children are asked to write about themselves, where they live, etc. The lessons present sentences as "statements" including a subject and a predicate without ever mentioning the technical terms. Within the first 50 lessons, my little ones have been able to write short paragraphs that describe familiar objects such as a ball, a cow, etc.

For another thing, the lessons are oh, so short! The instructions are usually one or two sentences long, and the exercise is not more than six to twelve short sentences (that follow a formula, so there is not that much thinking involved). If a child is focused, which is easy to do because of the simplicity, the longest lesson takes less than 15 minutes to complete!

Besides all this, the work is mostly self-directed. The learning is gradual, no great leaps are expected from one day to another, so little instruction or oversight is necessary. This is certainly a win/win for us moms of many! My children come away from the lessons feeling accomplished and energized without feeling frustrated. Before I realize it they are well on their way to being successful writers!

After I published a post on my blog recommending this resource, I realized there was a way to make things even easier (both for me and for my readers).

So, I finally sat down with some computer software and began the process of taking the original book and re-engineering it for modern use.

The result is what you see here. As an answer to prayer, I was able to come up with a way that streamlined the lessons and created a work text of sorts, with the original directions and copywork presented with places directly adjoining for the child to complete the work. **The instructions are included in each page—no extra searching, no lugging around a teacher's manual, no loss due to distraction between the printed page and the actual work.**

While I tried to keep to the flavor of the original work, I did tweak the lessons in a few areas, including some correction where the wording was a bit too archaic. I also restructured some of the composition lessons and even wrote a few to add that were more appropriate where necessary.

You will probably want to spend a minute or two on each lesson just to make sure the instructions are understood, and I would also check up to make sure they are done with neatness (remember, a little done well is better than a lot done poorly).

* Dictation lessons are repeated on the last few pages for your convenience.

Easy as pie, right?

Please note: You won't want your child to attempt this level until he/she has a good understanding of the different types of sentences and has a basic grasp of punctuation. If he is not used to these things, have him go through the first level of *Gentle Grammar* before you try this second level.

Blessings,

Sherry

P.S. For any further information on this or any other of our projects, please visit our site, momdelights.com

LANGUAGE EXERCISES
SECOND READER GRADE

Lesson 1

Copy these statements. How does each begin? How does each end?

1. The stars shine.

2. Grass grows in the field.

3. The rainbow is beautiful.

4. Cows are useful animals.

5. Leather is made from hides.

A sentence that tells or states something, is called a statement.

A statement begins with a capital letter.

A statement ends with a period.

LANGUAGE EXERCISES
SECOND READER GRADE

Lesson 2

These words are names of objects. Think about each object, and then write a statement, telling what you think.

1.	cow
2.	dog
3.	sled
4.	today
5.	mouse
6.	horse
7.	lady
8.	yesterday

LANGUAGE EXERCISES
SECOND READER GRADE

THE QUESTION

Lesson 3

Copy the following questions:

1.	Will the birds sing?
2.	Shall I help you?
3.	Can the horse run?
4.	Do stars twinkle?
5.	Are the leaves green?

A sentence that asks something is called a question.

A question begins with a capital letter.

A question ends with a question mark.

?

LANGUAGE EXERCISES
SECOND READER GRADE

	THE QUESTION
	Lesson 4
	Ask a question about:
1.	some fruit.
2.	some flower.
3.	the clouds.
4.	the weather.
	Write a question about:
1.	a cat
2.	a dog
3.	ice
4.	water

LANGUAGE EXERCISES
SECOND READER GRADE

	THE QUESTION
	Lesson 4 (continued)
5.	rain
6.	snow
7.	sky
8.	lesson

	DICTATION EXERCISE	
	The sky is blue.	The boy has a sled.
	Is the fire hot?	Does he have a pretty book?
	Do you know his name?	
1.		
2.		
3.		
4.		
5.		
	TO THE TEACHER: Read each sentence slowly. Do not repeat. These pages can be found on the last pages	

LANGUAGE EXERCISES
SECOND READER GRADE

MEMORY LESSON

Lesson 6. — *Copy and commit these lines.*

Work while you work, play while you play,

That is the way to be cheerful and gay!

All that you do, do with your might;

Things done by halves are never done right.

THE COMMAND

Lesson 7. — *Copy these sentences.*

1.	Lie down.
2.	Shut the door.
3.	Walk very softly
4.	Bring me the book.

LANGUAGE EXERCISES
SECOND READER GRADE

	THE COMMAND
	Lesson 7 (continued)
5.	Please open the window.
	A sentence which expresses an order is a *command*.
	Lesson 8.—*Make commands with these words.*
1.	books, close, your
2.	boys, the, let, sing
3.	fire, from, away, come, the
4.	mother, thy, honor, and, father
5.	pencil, the, desk, on, lay, the

LANGUAGE EXERCISES
SECOND READER GRADE

	Lesson 9.
1.	Write a command with a proper name for the first word; as *John*, come here.
2.	Write a command, using the name of one addressed for the last word; as, Be kind to your parents, *Charles*.
3.	Write a question, using a proper name of the last word; as, Are the roses in bloom, *Clara?*
4.	Give a command to Lucy, using her name in the middle of the sentence; as, Come, *Lucy*, or we will be late.
5.	Write a question with "Jane" for the first word; as, *Jane*, is the lily white as snow?

LANGUAGE EXERCISES
SECOND READER GRADE

	DICTATION EXERCISE
	Lesson 10. — *Cut off the top to use for the dictation.*
	1. Good morning, Edna.
	2. Pretty bird, come here.
	3. John, please walk slowly.
	4. See this pretty rose, Florence.
	5. Wait, Charles, for your sister.
	6. Did you have a pleasant walk, Sarah?
1.	
2.	
3.	
4.	
5.	
6.	
	TO THE TEACHER: Read each sentence slowly. Do not repeat. These pages can be found on the last pages.

LANGUAGE EXERCISES
SECOND READER GRADE

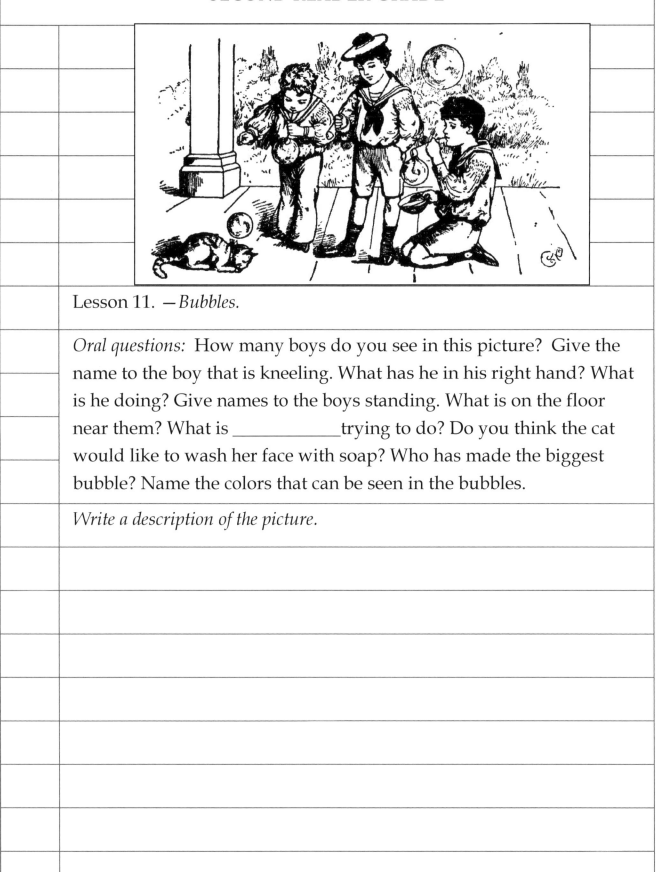

Lesson 11. —*Bubbles.*

Oral questions: How many boys do you see in this picture? Give the name to the boy that is kneeling. What has he in his right hand? What is he doing? Give names to the boys standing. What is on the floor near them? What is _____trying to do? Do you think the cat would like to wash her face with soap? Who has made the biggest bubble? Name the colors that can be seen in the bubbles.

Write a description of the picture.

LANGUAGE EXERCISES
SECOND READER GRADE

THE COMMA

Lesson 12. — A comma separates three or more words used in the same way; as, Charles can see, hear, and feel.

Place commas in these sentences where they should be.

1. | The pear is large yellow and juicy.

2. | Mary reads writes and sings well.

THE MONTHS

Lesson 13. — *Copy the names of the months.*

January	
February	
March	
April	
May	
June	
July	
August	
September	
October	
November	
December	

LANGUAGE EXERCISES
SECOND READER GRADE

WINTER JEWELS

Lesson 14. — *Place commas in these sentences where they should be.*

Spring summer autumn and winter are seasons.

March April and May are the spring months.

September October and November are autumn months.

Thanksgiving Day Christmas New Year's Day and Fourth of July are holidays.

Lesson 15. — *Write answers.*

1. How many seasons are there?

2. What are the names of the seasons?

3. In which season do we have the warmest weather?

4. In which the coldest weather?

5. When is the weather mild or temperate?

LANGUAGE EXERCISES
SECOND READER GRADE

THE SEASONS

Lesson 16. *Commit the lines. Write them from memory.*

A million little diamonds
Twinkled in the trees,
And all the little maidens said:
"A jewel, if you please!"

But while they held their hands outstretched
To catch the diamonds gay,
A million little sunbeams came
And snatched them all away.

LANGUAGE EXERCISES
SECOND READER GRADE

WINTER JEWELS

Lesson 16. (continued)

1.	
2.	
3.	
4.	
5.	
6.	
7.	
8.	

LANGUAGE EXERCISES
SECOND READER GRADE

A AND AN

Lesson 17. — *Write sentences containing these words.*

1.	an ax
2.	an apple
3.	an eye
4.	an ear
5.	an inkstand
6.	an iron ring
7.	an ox
8.	an overcoat
	Examples: The man has an apple. Do you have an apple?

LANGUAGE EXERCISES
SECOND READER GRADE

A AND AN

Lesson 18. —*Write the words, using "a" or "an" before each.*

	hat		book
	house		inch
	ear ring		egg
	hour		uncle
	echo		newspaper
	owl		island
	orange		elbow
	umbrella		

Doodle here:

LANGUAGE EXERCISES
SECOND READER GRADE

	THIS, THERE; THAT, THOSE
	Lesson 19. — *When we speak of one we may use "this" or "that"; when we speak of more than one, "these" or "those." Change "this" in these sentences to "these," and write the sentences correctly.*
1.	This man is old.
2.	This boy was skating.
3.	This lady has a bonnet.
4.	This box has a lid.
5.	You may eat this cherry.
6.	Was this fly on the wall?
7.	Give this woman some money.
8.	This goose has white wings.

LANGUAGE EXERCISES
SECOND READER GRADE

	THIS, THERE; THAT, THOSE
	Lesson 20. — *Change "that" to "those" in writing these sentences.*
1.	That ox has horns.
2.	Hand me that loaf.
3.	That knife has blades.
4.	Where is that potato?
5.	That church is beautiful.
6.	Does that mouse have bright eyes?
7.	Where was that house with large windows?
8.	Was that tomato in the garden?

LANGUAGE EXERCISES
SECOND READER GRADE

Lesson 21. — Fill each of the following blanks with one of these words:
"Are," "has," "is," "have," "were," "was."

1. There _____ a star in the sky.

2. There _____ flowers in the garden

3. There _____ apples on the tree last summer.

4. There _____ been no one here.

5. There _____ been many stormy days.

6. There _____ the happy children.

7. There _____ grass in the field.

8. There _____ an orange in the box.

9. There _____ ships on the water.

LANGUAGE EXERCISES
SECOND READER GRADE

Lesson 22, — *Write these sentences correctly, using "they" for "he," "she," or "it"; as, He is my classmate, They are my classmates.*

1.	He is in school.
2.	She is a member of our class.
3.	Is he a merchant?
4.	Does she have a new book?
5.	It roars like a lion.
6.	He was very studious.
7.	Is it a bird of prey?
8.	She was in Boston last summer.

LANGUAGE EXERCISES
SECOND READER GRADE

	Lesson 22. (continued)
9.	Has he been to Newport?
10.	Has she seen the swan?
	Doodle space:

Lesson 23. — *Write the names of all the things you see in the picture; write a question and its answer about each object.*

LANGUAGE EXERCISES
SECOND READER GRADE

	Lesson 23 (continued)
1.	
Q.	
A,	
2.	
Q.	
A.	
3.	
Q.	
A.	
4.	
Q.	
A.	
5.	
Q.	
A.	
6.	
Q.	
A.	

LANGUAGE EXERCISES
SECOND READER GRADE

Lesson 23. (continued)

Write a story from the picture, using the following hints.

The little boy and girl that you see in the picture are brother and sister. Do they live in the city or in the country? What is the name of the boy? What is the name of the girl? How old is ____? How old is ____? Who is the man in front of them? What do you suppose he carries in the bag? What will he give the children?

LANGUAGE EXERCISES
SECOND READER GRADE

WORDS THAT DENOTE POSSESSION

Lesson 24. — *Copy the statements. When you use a word denoting the owner, do not forget the little apostrophe (').*

1.	This is John's slate.
2.	Mary's lamb is white.
3.	The duck's bill is broad.
4.	The dog's name is Bose.
5.	The bird's nest is in the tree.

LANGUAGE EXERCISES
SECOND READER GRADE

WORDS THAT DENOTE POSSESSION

Lesson 25. — *Think who owns each thing named, and write answers to these questions.*

1.	Whose slate is this?
2.	Whose table is this?
3.	Whose desk is that?
4.	Whose book is on the desk?
5.	Whose hats are in the closet?
6.	Whose ring is on her finger?

LANGUAGE EXERCISES
SECOND READER GRADE

MEMORY LESSON

Lesson 26. — *Copy and commit these lines.*

1. When doubtful which is right, which wrong,

2. This you can safely do:

3. Do unto others as you would

4. That they should do to you.

LANGUAGE EXERCISES
SECOND READER GRADE

Lesson 27.

How many boys are shown in this picture? Do you think they are brothers? What are the boys doing? Is the larger boy kind to the smaller one? Why do you think so? What is back of the boys? Whose home do you think it is? Is there a fire in the house? What do you see that makes you think so? Is it summer or winter? What shows you this? Is it a sunny or cloudy day? How do you know? What else do you see in the picture? Where are the chickens?

Describe the picture, using the questions as a guide. Then close the book and describe the picture from memory.

Lesson 28. — *"Has," "have," and "had" are used with "seen"; they are not used with, "saw." Place the proper words in these blanks.*

I _____ seen.   He _____ seen.

You _____ seen.   We _____ seen.

They _____ seen.

Fill the blanks in the following sentences with "saw," "has," "have," or "had."

Rose _____ the white rabbit.

Charles _____ seen Ann's pet.

_____ you seen the little chicks?

_____ the children seen their presents?

LANGUAGE EXERCISES
SECOND READER GRADE

Lesson 29.

Write two sentences about objects in this room. Use the word "see" in each.

1.

2.

Write two sentences about something you observed this morning. Use the word *saw* in each.

1.

2.

LANGUAGE EXERCISES
SECOND READER GRADE

	THE QUESTION
	Lesson 29. (continued)
	Write three sentences, using:
	have seen has seen had seen
1.	
2.	
3.	

WENT, HAS GONE, HAVE GONE, HAD GONE

	Lesson 30. — *"Has," "have," and "had" should not be used with "went." Supply the proper words in these blanks.*
1.	I _____ gone.
2.	You _____ gone.
3.	He _____ gone.
4.	Mary _____ gone to school.
5.	The boys _____gone fishing.
6.	_____the ducks gone to the river?

LANGUAGE EXERCISES
SECOND READER GRADE

Lesson 31. — *Write these sentences, changing "has" to "have."*

1.	The child has gone to play.
2.	The man has gone to work.
3.	Has he gone to dinner?
4.	Has the woman gone home?
5.	The ox has gone to the pasture.
6.	Has she gone to market?
7.	The lady has gone to the store.
8.	The bird has gone to its nest.
9.	Has the horse gone to the stable?

LANGUAGE EXERCISES
SECOND READER GRADE

DID, HAS DONE, HAVE DONE, HAD DONE.

Lesson 32. — *Use "has," or "had" with "done." Place the proper words in these blanks.*

1.	I _____ done.
2.	You _____ done.
3.	He _____ done.
4.	We _____ done.
5.	They _____ done.
6.	I _____ done what you bid.
7.	He _____ done his task.
8.	The exercise _____ done him good.
9.	The men _____ done their work.
10.	You _____ done well, John.

LANGUAGE EXERCISES
SECOND READER GRADE

Lesson 33. — *Form sentences, each containing one of the following phrases.*

1.	have seen
2.	have gone
3.	have done
4.	has seen
5.	has gone
6.	has done
7.	had seen
8.	had gone
9.	had done

LANGUAGE EXERCISES
SECOND READER GRADE

	HOW TO WRITE INITIALS
	Lesson 34. — *The first letter of a name is called an initial; as, J. A. G. are the initials of James Abram Garfield; U. S. of the United States. Write the initials of your own name. Write the initials of these names.*
1.	Chester Alan Arthur
2.	William Cullen Bryant
3.	Ulysses Simpson Grant
4.	Oliver Wendell Holmes
5.	Henry Wadsworth Longfellow
	THEIR, THERE
	Lesson 35. — *Write sentences containing these words. The word "their" is always used with the name of some object.*
1.	their hats
2.	their coats
3.	their books
4.	their slates

LANGUAGE EXERCISES
SECOND READER GRADE

	Lesson 35. (continued)
5.	their balls
6.	their bonnets
	Write two or more sentences containing the word "there."
1.	
2.	
3.	
	Doodle space:

LANGUAGE EXERCISES
SECOND READER GRADE

DICTATION EXERCISE.

Lesson 36.

1.	There are birds on that tree.
2.	See them feed their young.
3.	Mary and Annie live there.
4.	Their pony has a beautiful mane.

1.	
2.	
3.	
4.	

LANGUAGE EXERCISES
SECOND READER GRADE

	Lesson 37. — *Use one of these words correctly in each of the following blanks: "flour," "flower," "week," "weak," "threw," "through."*
1.	We use _____ to make bread.
2.	William gave her a pretty _____.
3.	The child is too _____ to sit up.
4.	Is Saturday the last day of the _____?
5.	He walked _____ to the park.
6.	George _____ the stone _____ the window.
	Lesson 38. — *Insert the proper word in each of the following blunks: "cells," "sells," "seize," "sees," "buy," "by," "scent," "sent," "cent."*
1.	Bees put honey in _____.
2.	The merchant _____ his goods.
3.	The lion will _____ his prey.
4.	The child _____ the bright star.
5.	We _____ peaches _____ the peck.
6.	The _____ of flower is pleasant.
7.	He was _____ to the store with a _____.

LANGUAGE EXERCISES
SECOND READER GRADE

QUOTATION MARKS

Lesson 39. — *Copy these sentences. Mind the inverted quotation marks when they begin to speak and when they end.*

1.	"Name the parts of an orange," said Ida.
2.	"It has a peel, pulp, and seeds," said Clara.

The little marks that enclose the exact words of what someone says are called *quotation marks*.

Lesson 40. — *Copy these lines using quotation marks.*

1.	When I go to bed I say, "Good night."
2.	When I get up I say, "Good morning."
3.	I always say, "Thank you."
4.	Polite boys and girls say, "If you please."

LANGUAGE EXERCISES
SECOND READER GRADE

	Lesson 40. — *Copy these lines, using quotation marks.*
1.	When I go to bed I say, "Good night."
2.	When I get up I say, "Good morning."
3.	I always say, "Thank you."
4.	Polite boys and girls say, "If you please."
	DICTATION EXERCISE
	Lesson 41.
	It is Frank's pencil. It is made partly of wood. It is brown, long, round, and sharp. Joe said, "Frank's pencil has a very sharp point."
1.	
2.	
3.	
4.	

LANGUAGE EXERCISES
SECOND READER GRADE

Lesson 42. — *The Bird's Nest. Copy this story, then cover it up and write it from memory. Use quotation marks to show what Mary said.*

Mary found a bird's nest with two pretty eggs in it. The birds flew around her head, making loud cries. Mary said, "Don't be afraid, little birds, I'll not touch your nest."

LANGUAGE EXERCISES
SECOND READER GRADE

MEMORY LESSON.

Lesson 43. — *Commit to memory these lines.*

Don't rob the birds of their eggs, boys,
    It is cruel, and heartless, and wrong;
But remember, by breaking an egg, boys,
    We may lose a bird with a song.

Lesson 44. — *The Dog in the Manger.*

A dog was lying in a manger. A hungry ox saw the hay in the manger and wanted to eat it. The dog barked and snapped at the ox, and would not let him touch it.

The ox said, "You are a selfish dog, for you can not eat the hay, and you will not allow others to eat it."

What do you call a story of this kind? What is a fable? Write in your own words the story of The Dog in the Manger.

LANGUAGE EXERCISES
SECOND READER GRADE

Lesson 45. — *The Toad.* *

Did you ever see a toad?

I had one in my yard, and what do you think he liked to eat? Bread? Oh, no. Milk? No, he liked spiders.

If I put a spider near him, out came the toad's tongue, and into his mouth went the spider. You and I do not like spiders, but my toad would eat forty or fifty for his diner.

Write the story of the toad.

* TO THE TEACHER. — In a conversation lesson give information on the following points about the toad: where usually found; what doing there; its food; how it catches it; the sticky substance covering the tongue, by means of which it holds fast any insect that touches it.

LANGUAGE EXERCISES
SECOND READER GRADE

THE QUESTION

Lesson 46. — *The Bee.*

MEMORY LESSON

How does the little busy bee
    Improve each shining hour,
And gather honey all the day
    From every opening flower!

How skillfully she builds her cell,
    How neat she spreads her wax;
And labors hard to store it well
    With the sweet food she makes.

LANGUAGE EXERCISES
SECOND READER GRADE

	Lesson 46. — (continued)
1,	At what season of the year do we see the bee?
2.	Where?
3.	What is it doing all summer?
4.	Why do bees make so much honey?
5.	Where do bees live?
6.	What would happen if we disturbed them?
	Doodle space:

LANGUAGE EXERCISES
SECOND READER GRADE

Lesson 47. — *The Apple.*

1. On what kind of tree does the apple grow?

2. What shape is an apple?

3, What color is an apple?

4. What is the white part called?

5. What color are the seeds when the apple is ripe?

6. For what are apples used?

LANGUAGE EXERCISES
SECOND READER GRADE

	Lesson 48. — *The Shoe.*
1.	Who makes shoes?
2.	Of what are shoes made?
3.	Tell in a sentence the name of the part on the ground.
4.	Tell in a sentence the part that covers the top and sides of the foot.
5.	Of what use are shoes?

LANGUAGE EXERCISES
SECOND READER GRADE

Lesson 49. — *The Rose.*

1.	What is the rose?
2.	What is its color?
3.	On what does it grow?
4.	In what places have you seen the rose growing?
5.	Why do we like the rose?
	Doodle here:

LANGUAGE EXERCISES
SECOND READER GRADE

Lesson 50. — *Iron.*

1. Tell something that is made of iron.

2. How does the iron feel?

3. When you try to lift it, what would you say it is?

4. Where do we get iron?

5. Of what use is it?

Doodle space:

LANGUAGE EXERCISES
SECOND READER GRADE

	Lesson 51. — *Gold.*
1.	What is the color of gold?
3.	Where is it found?
4.	Name four things that are made of gold.
5.	Which one of them are useful?
6.	Which beautiful?
	Lesson 52. — *The Baker.*
1.	What does the baker make?
2.	Of what is bread made?
3.	Where is the bread baked?

LANGUAGE EXERCISES
SECOND READER GRADE

Lesson 53. — *The Cunning Cat.*

The cunning old cat lay down on a mat
        By the fire in the oaken hall;
"If the little mice peep, they'll think I'm asleep,"
        So she rolled herself up like a ball.

Nibble, nibble, nibble! When the little mice,
        And they licked their little paws;
Then the cunning old cat sprang up from the mat,
        And caught them all with her claws.

Use each of these words in a sentence.

1.	mice
2.	paws
3.	oaken
4.	claws
5.	asleep
6.	rolled

	Lesson 53. — (continued)
7.	sprang
8.	little
9.	nibble
10.	caught
11.	licked
12.	cunning
	Doodle here:

LANGUAGE EXERCISES
SECOND READER GRADE

	COLORS
	Lesson 54. — *Primary Colors.*
1.	What color is the clear sky?
2.	What is the color of blood?
3.	What is the color of butter?
4.	What kind of colors are blue, yellow, and red?
	Lesson 55.
1.	Write the names of six colors.
2.	Which are the primary colors?
3.	Which are the secondary colors?
4.	What colors make purple?

LANGUAGE EXERCISES
SECOND READER GRADE

	THE QUESTION
	Lesson 56.
5.	What colors make green?
6.	What colors make orange?
7.	What colors have you seen in fruit?
8.	What colors have you seen in flowers?
9.	What colors have you seen in birds?
10.	What colors have you seen in the sunset?
11.	What colors have you seen in the rainbow?

MEMORY LESSON.

Lesson 57. — *A Child's Prayer.*

I thank thee, Lord, for quiet rest,
    And for they care of me;
Oh, let me through this day be blest,
    And kept from harm by thee.

Oh, let me thank thee; kind thou art,
    To children such as I:
Give me a gentle, loving heart;
    Be Thou my Friend on high.

Help me to please my parents dear,
    And do whate'er they tell;
Bless all my friends, both far and near,
    And keep them safe and well.

LANGUAGE EXERCISES
SECOND READER GRADE

LETTER WRITING

Lesson 58. — *A Letter.*

Copy this letter on another piece of paper or in a notebook. Notice the use of capitals and marks of punctuation, and the arrangement of different parts. Copy the letter again, using the name of one of your friends, and sign your own name.

May 4, 1889

Dear Clara,

Tomorrow is my ninth birthday, and mother says I can have a party in the afternoon.

Brother Frank will put up a swing for us. I have a new set of dishes, and we will have a tea party in the back yard. Will you come? We expect to have a very good time.

Your friend,

Samantha

LANGUAGE EXERCISES
SECOND READER GRADE

Lesson 59. — *Addresses. Copy these envelopes.*

Mr. Charles Bond
425 Euclid Ave.
Denver, CO 80201

Miss Cora Innes
2305 Wyoming Blvd.
Dallas, TX 75205

LANGUAGE EXERCISES
SECOND READER GRADE

Lesson 60. — *Address these envelopes for these different people.*

1. Yourself.

2, Your father.

3. Your mother.

LANGUAGE EXERCISES
SECOND READER GRADE

LANGUAGE EXERCISES
SECOND READER GRADE

DICTATION LESSONS FOR PARENTS TO READ ALOUD

Dictation lesson 4.

The sky is blue.	The boy has a sled.
Is the fire hot?	Does he have a pretty book?
Do you know his name?	

Dictation lesson 10.

1. Good morning, Edna.

2. Pretty bird, come here.

3. John, please walk slowly.

4. See this pretty rose, Florence.

5. Wait, Charles, for your sister.

6. Did you have a pleasant walk, Sarah?

Dictation lesson 41.

It is Frank's pencil. It is made partly of wood. It is brown, long, round, and sharp. Joe said, "Frank's pencil has a very sharp point."

LANGUAGE EXERCISES
SECOND READER GRADE

LANGUAGE EXERCISES
SECOND READER GRADE

Made in the USA
Coppell, TX
01 September 2021